desserts

igloo

igloo

Published by Igloo Books Ltd
Cottage Farm
Sywell
NN6 0BJ
www.igloo-books.com

10 9 8 7 6 5 4 3 2

ISBN: 978 1 84817 632 4

Project Managed by R&R Publications Marketing Pty Ltd

Food Photography: R&R Photostudio (www.rrphotostudio.com.au)
Recipe Development: R&R Test Kitchen

Front cover photograph © Stockfood/Jean Cazals

Printed and manufactured in India

contents

introduction

Puddings are the icing on the cake, as the saying goes. They certainly make a meal seem special, no matter what the occasion – tonight's family dinner or a special celebration.

This compendium of sweet courses includes old-fashioned favourites as well as many exciting new ways to conclude the evening meal. They're all designed to make that last course the one the family looks forward to most.

Even with today's busy lifestyle, there's no need to drop dessert from everyday meals when you have these easy and economical, delights to choose from. As summer's bounty ripens, offer your family baked treats filled with the heady fragrances and flavours of fresh fruit. Or choose a sorbet or ice cream – so sophisticated in flavour, yet child's play to create.

At the first sign of cold weather, turn your thoughts to warm, soul-satisfying steamed puddings, hot pies, cobblers and custards. They're sure to to raise the family's spirits on chilly nights.

And when it's time for a dinner party dazzler, look through our irresistible temptations to delight your guests. Whatever your preference – sweet and spicy, fruit-filled, frozen or flambéed – you're sure to find the perfect finale.

simple treats

Fresh Mango and Mascarpone Brûlée

(see photograph on page 6)

4 large ripe mangoes

250g tub mascarpone

200g tub Greek yoghurt

1½ teaspoon dried ground ginger

finely grated rind and juice of 1 lime

1 tablespoon dark or light rum (optional)

6 tablespoon light muscovado sugar

20g unsalted butter

fresh mint to decorate (optional)

1 Peel the mangoes, using a vegetable peeler, then slice the flesh off the stone and chop, collecting any juices in a bowl.

2 Whisk together the mascarpone and yoghurt using a whisk or a fork, then stir in the ginger, lime rind and juice. Whisk in the rum, if using.

3 Place the mango and juices in a deep 18cm ovenproof dish, or divide between 6 ovenproof ramekins. Spoon over the mascarpone mixture, then sprinkle over the sugar and dot with the butter. Refrigerate until required.

4 Preheat the grill to high. Grill the dessert for 4–5 minutes in the dish or 1–2 minutes in the ramekins, until lightly golden and bubbling. Cool for 1–2 minutes, then decorate with mint, if using.

Serves 6

Double Mango and Yoghurt Cups

(see photograph opposite)

145ml carton double cream

400g can mango slices in syrup, drained

200g plain yoghurt

1 teaspoon vanilla extract

1 ripe mango

1 Whip the cream until it just forms soft peaks. Blend the mango slices to a thick purée in a food processor or press through a sieve. Mix the purée with the yoghurt until thoroughly combined, then fold in the whipped cream and vanilla extract.

2 Slice off the 2 fat sides of the mango, close to the stone. Cut a criss-cross pattern across the flesh (but not the skin) of 1 side with a sharp knife. Push the skin inside out to expose the flesh and cut the cubes off. Peel the other side and slice thinly.

3 Fold the mango cubes into the mango mixture, reserving the slices. Divide the mixture between serving bowls, cover and refrigerate for 2 hours. Serve decorated with the reserved mango slices.

Serves 4

Caramelised Banana Pancakes

1 large egg

100g plain flour, sifted

pinch of salt

1 cup semi-skimmed milk

30g butter, melted sunflower oil
  for greasing

2 large, firm bananas, sliced

3 tablespoons Madeira, dessert wine or
  2 tablespoons Drambuie

2–3 teaspoons raw sugar

1 Beat the egg, flour, salt and a little milk to form a smooth paste. Gradually mix in the remaining milk, then stir in the butter.

2 Brush a non-stick, medium-sized frying pan with the oil and heat until very hot. Pour in 2–3 tablespoons of batter, swirling to cover the base of the pan. Cook the pancakes for 1–2 minutes each side, until golden. Repeat to make 7 more, keeping the pancakes warm and layering them between sheets of baking paper to stop them sticking.

3 Preheat the grill to high. Wipe the pan, add the bananas and Madeira, wine or Drambuie and heat through gently, stirring.

4 When most of the liquid has evaporated, place a spoonful of the banana mixture on each pancake, fold it into quarters and place in a flameproof dish. Sprinkle with the sugar and grill until the tops of the pancakes are golden and lightly caramelised.

Serves 4

Note: These pancakes filled with hot gooey bananas have a hidden kick! For children, you can replace the alcohol with the maple syrup. Serve with Greek yoghurt or ice cream.

Warm Apricot Brioches

4 individual brioches

6 fresh apricots, halved and stoned, or
  12 canned apricot halves, drained

½ cup apricot conserve or jam

1 tablespoon orange juice

4 small scoops vanilla ice cream

1 Preheat the oven to 180°C. Slice the top off each brioche and reserve, then carefully hollow out the centres and discard. Place 3 apricot halves in the middle of each brioche.

2 Put the brioches and their tops onto a baking sheet and cook for 8 minutes or until heated through and slightly crispy. Meanwhile, gently heat the conserve or jam in a saucepan with the orange juice, stirring, until melted.

3 Place each brioche on a plate and top with a scoop of ice cream. Drizzle the conserve or jam mixture over, then replace the tops.

Serves 4

Glazed Apples in Brandy Snap Baskets

2 large eating apples, peeled, cored and thickly sliced

30g butter

1 tablespoon caster sugar

2 tablespoons brandy or Calvados (optional)

2 tablespoons lemon curd

½ cup crème fraîche

6 brandy snap baskets

thin strips lemon zest, pared with a vegetable peeler, to decorate

1 Place the apples in a saucepan with the butter, sugar and brandy or Calvados, (if using). Simmer for 5 minutes or until the apples have softened.

2 Mix together the lemon curd and crème fraîche, then divide between the brandy snap baskets. Spoon the apple mixture over, decorate with the lemon zest and serve immediately.

Serves 6

Honeyed Figs with Mascarpone

12–16 fresh figs, depending on size

2 tablespoons clear honey

1 tablespoon pine nut kernels

85g mascarpone

1 Preheat the oven to 180°C. Cut a deep cross into each fig at the stalk end, then open out slightly. Place the figs close together in an ovenproof dish to keep them upright.

2 Drizzle the honey over and inside the figs, then cook for 10 minutes, until soft. Meanwhile, place a frying pan over a medium heat and dry-fry the pine nuts for 2 minutes, stirring often, until golden.

3 Transfer 3–4 figs to each serving plate, scatter the pine nuts around them and serve with a spoonful of mascarpone.

Serves 4

Strawberry Trifle Brûlée

85g amaretti biscuits, roughly crushed, or 2 trifle sponges, halved

3 tablespoons Madeira, sweet sherry or Kirsch

85ml whipping or double cream

85ml ready-made custard

85g strawberries, hulled and halved

3 tablespoons raw sugar

1 Divide the biscuits or sponge halves between 4 x 150ml ramekins and spoon over the Madeira, sherry or Kirsch.

2 Whip the cream until it forms soft peaks, then fold in the custard and strawberries. Divide the cream mixture between the ramekins. Smooth the tops and sprinkle over a thick layer of sugar.

3 Meanwhile, preheat the grill to high (190°C). Place the ramekins under the grill for 2–3 minutes, until the sugar caramelises. Leave to cool, then refrigerate for 2 hours before serving.

Serves 4

Peach and Hazelnut Crumble

3 x 400g cans peach halves in natural juice, drained but reserving

200ml of juice

3 pieces preserved ginger in syrup, drained and finely chopped

85g plain flour

85g roasted chopped hazelnuts

5 tablespoons soft light brown sugar

1 teaspoon ground cinnamon

85g butter, cubed

1 Preheat the oven to 200°C. Arrange the peaches, cut-side up, in a 30 x 25cm ovenproof dish. Sprinkle with the ginger. Boil the reserved juice in a saucepan for 5 minutes or until reduced by ⅓. Pour over the peaches.

2 In a large bowl, mix together the flour, hazelnuts, sugar and cinnamon. Rub in the butter with the tips of your fingers until the mixture resembles fine breadcrumbs. Sprinkle over the fruit and bake for 30–35 minutes, until browned.

Serves 6

Banana Filo Tart

6 large sheets filo pastry, defrosted if
  frozen, trimmed to 25 x 30cm

55g unsalted butter, melted

3 large bananas, sliced

4 dried figs, sliced

30g caster sugar

pinch of ground apple spice

grated zest of 1 lemon

1 tablespoon dark rum

1 Preheat the oven to 200°C. Place a baking sheet on the top shelf to heat.

2 Brush a sheet of filo pastry with butter. Top with a second sheet and brush
   it with butter. Repeat with the remaining sheets until all the pastry has been
   used, then transfer to a cold baking sheet.

3 Arrange the banana and fig slices over the pastry sheets, then scatter over
   the sugar, apple spice and lemon zest. Pour the rum and any remaining butter
   over. Carefully transfer the tart to the heated baking sheet using a fish slice
   and bake for 15 minutes or until golden and bubbling.

Serves 4

The Easiest Apple Pie Ever

250g plain flour

125g butter, cubed

2 tablespoons apricot jelly

500g cooking apples, peeled, cored and thinly sliced

1 teaspoon ground cinnamon

½ teaspoon apple spice

finely grated zest of 1 orange

55g soft light brown sugar

55g sultanas

icing sugar to dust

1 Preheat the oven to 190°C. Put the flour into a bowl and rub in the butter until the mixture resembles fine breadcrumbs. Add enough cold water (about 3–4 tablespoons) to make a smooth dough. Knead very lightly.

2 Roll out the pastry to a 35cm round on a lightly floured surface. Place on a large baking sheet. Spread the jelly over the centre of the pastry. In a bowl, toss together the apples, cinnamon, apple spice, orange zest, sugar and golden raisins, then pile the mixture into the middle of the pastry. Bring the edges of the pastry up over the apple mixture, pressing into rough pleats but leaving the centre of the pie open.

3 Bake for 35–45 minutes, until the pastry is golden, covering the pie with foil if the apple starts to burn. Remove the foil (if using), then sprinkle over the icing sugar before serving.

Serves 4

Fig and Hazelnut Tart

55g roasted chopped hazelnuts

370g ready-rolled puff pastry sheet

55g unsalted butter, softened

3 tablespoons caster sugar

½ teaspoon ground cinnamon

8 large ripe figs, sliced

1 Preheat the oven to 220°C. Place a baking sheet on the middle shelf to heat.

2 Grind the hazelnuts in a food processor or with a pestle and mortar. Unroll the pastry sheet and trim to 23cm square. Mix the butter, hazelnuts, ⅔ of the sugar and the cinnamon with a fork to form a paste. Spread the paste over the pastry leaving the edges clear.

3 Arrange the figs on top of the hazelnut paste, then sprinkle with the remaining sugar. Transfer to the heated baking sheet and bake for 15 minutes or until the pastry is puffed up and golden.

Serves 4

Note: A rich hazelnut paste is spread over puff pastry then topped with sliced fresh figs before being baked until golden. It's delicious with mascarpone or crème fraîche.

Rum and Lime Banana Fritters

4 bananas

juice of 1 lime

2 teaspoons caster sugar

1 tablespoon dark rum

oil for deep-frying

BATTER

125g plain flour

1/4 teaspoon baking powder

pinch of salt

145ml water

2 tablespoons sesame seeds

1   Peel each banana and cut in half crossways, then slice lengthways to make quarters. Place the banana quarters, lime juice, sugar and rum in a deep, non-metallic dish and mix gently. Cover and set aside for at least 30 minutes to marinate.

2   Meanwhile, make the batter. Sift the flour and salt into a mixing bowl. Pour in 145ml of water and whisk to form a smooth, thick batter. Stir in the sesame seeds and set aside.

3   Heat 5cm of oil in a wok or a large, deep frying pan until smoking hot. Coat the banana pieces thoroughly in the batter. Fry for 5 minutes or until golden brown, then turn over and cook for 2 minutes to brown the other side (you may have to cook them in batches). Drain on kitchen towels.

Serves 4

Note: These hot banana fritters are wonderful on their own, but if you serve them with a scoop of good-quality vanilla ice cream, they become totally irresistible.

Cantuccini Biscuit and Fruit Trifle

200g cantuccini biscuits or biscotti

3 tablespoons espresso or other strong, good quality coffee, cooled

2 tablespoons brandy

1 tablespoon caster sugar

125g strawberries, hulled and quartered

125g seedless grapes, halved

2 small bananas, sliced and tossed in lemon juice

30g semi sweet chocolate, grated

1¾ cups whipping cream

1 Place the cantuccini or biscotti in a plastic bag. Seal, then roughly crush with a rolling pin. Put half the crushed biscuits into a shallow dish, add the coffee, brandy and sugar and set aside for 10 minutes to let the liquid soak into the biscuits.

2 Spoon the fruit over the soaked biscuits and scatter over half the chocolate.

3 Whisk the cream until it holds its shape. Spoon over the fruit and chocolate. Top with the remaining crushed biscuits and chocolate.

Serves 4

Note: Make the coffee ahead of time and allow it to cool. This very rich dessert can be served immediately but does benefit from chilling – so make it in advance if possible.

Hazelnut Meringue in Raspberry Sorbet

285g meringue mix

55g roasted chopped hazelnuts

2 teaspoons cornflour

200ml crème fraîche

100g fresh raspberries

fresh mint to decorate

SORBET

250g fresh or frozen raspberries, defrosted if frozen

1 ripe banana, mashed

juice of 1 orange

1 First make the sorbet. Beat the raspberries with the banana and orange juice until thoroughly combined. Transfer to a freezer container and freeze for 2–3 hours, stirring 1–2 times.

2 Preheat the oven to 150°C. Line 2 baking sheets with baking paper. Prepare the meringue mix according to the packet instructions, whisking until it forms stiff peaks (this is best done with an electric whisk).

3 Fold in the hazelnuts and cornflour. Spoon the mixture onto the baking sheets, making 3 circles on each. Swirl the tops with a fork to flatten, then cook for 1 hour or until crisp. Cool for 20 minutes.

4 Top the meringues with the crème fraîche. Place small balls or curls of the sorbet on top with the raspberries and decorate with the fresh mint.

Serves 6

Note: The slight tartness of the raspberry sorbet really livens up this beautiful pudding. You can make the sorbet a week in advance, but defrost it for 15 minutes before serving.

summer and autumn fruits

Creamy Raspberry Fool

(see photograph on page 24)

350g fresh raspberries

55g caster sugar

200ml carton crème fraîche

1 Reserve a few raspberries for decoration, then mix the rest with ½ the sugar and press the mixture through a sieve. Stir in the remaining sugar to taste.

2 Place the crème fraîche in a large bowl and gently fold in the raspberry purée until combined. Spoon into small coffee cups or glasses and refrigerate for 2–3 hours to firm up slightly. Serve decorated with the reserved raspberries.

Serves 4

Note: This fool is so simple to make, yet it's special enough to serve at any dinner party. Don't put the raspberries on top too far in advance - they might start to sink.

Summer Pudding with Redcurrant Sauce

(see photograph opposite)

1 kg fresh or frozen mixed berry fruits

3 tablespoons caster sugar

8 slices white or wholemeal bread, crusts removed

2 tablespoons redcurrant jelly

1 Place the fruit, sugar and 3 tablespoons of water in a saucepan and simmer for 5 minutes or until the fruit has softened. Leave to cool slightly.

2 Line the base and sides of a large pudding basin with 6 slices of the bread, cutting them to fit and making sure there are no gaps. Strain the fruit, reserving the juice, then add the fruit to the basin. Cover with the remaining bread to form a lid. Spoon over 3–4 tablespoons of the reserved juice.

3 Place a plate on top of the bread, with a weight (such as a large can) on it. Place in the fridge for 2–3 hours to let the juices soak through the bread.

4 To make the sauce, strain the reserved juice into a pan, then add the redcurrant jelly. Simmer for 2–3 minutes, stirring, until the jelly has melted. Invert the pudding onto a plate and serve with the redcurrant sauce.

Serves 6

Note: This is many people's favourite pudding. It's easy to make and healthy too. However, it just doesn't taste the same without at least 1 spoonful of whipped cream.

Blueberry and Apple Oatmeal Crumble

75g plain wholemeal flour

55g medium oatmeal

30g ground almonds

55g margarine

55g soft light brown sugar

1 teaspoon ground cinnamon

3 apples, peeled, cored and thinly sliced

250g fresh blueberries

2 tablespoons unsweetened apple juice

1 tablespoon clear honey

1 Preheat the oven to 180°C. Place the flour, oatmeal and almonds in a bowl and stir to mix. Lightly rub in the margarine until the mixture resembles breadcrumbs. Stir in the sugar and cinnamon.

2 Place the apples and blueberries in a 16 x 23cm ovenproof dish. Mix together the apple juice and honey, pour over the apples and blueberries and stir gently to mix.

3 Spoon the crumble mixture evenly over the fruit so that it is completely covered. Bake for 40–45 minutes, until golden brown.

Serves 4

Note: You can raspberries or sliced peaches instead of blueberries in this crunchy, fruit-packed crumble. Serve it with low-fat custard, plain yoghurt or ice cream

Strawberry and Cream Tartlets

145g plain flour

1 tablespoon caster sugar, plus extra
to dust

100g unsalted butter, softened

finely grated zest of 1 small lemon, plus
1 teaspoon juice

145ml double or whipping cream

250g strawberries, halved

4 tablespoons raspberry jam or
redcurrant jam to glaze

1 Preheat the oven to 190°C. Sift the flour and sugar into a bowl. Rub in the
butter and the lemon juice and knead lightly until the mixture forms a smooth
dough. Cover with plastic wrap and refrigerate for 15 minutes.

2 Roll the dough out thinly on a lightly floured surface, divide it into 4 and use
it to line 4 x 7½cm loose-bottomed tartlet tins. Line with baking paper and
baking beans and bake for 15 minutes. Remove the paper and beans and
cook for another 3–5 minutes, until the pastry is golden. Leave to cool for
15 minutes, then remove from the tins.

3 Whip the cream with the lemon zest until it forms soft peaks. Spoon into the
cases and top with the strawberries. Melt the selected jam over a gentle
heat with 1 tablespoon of water, then press through a sieve and cool slightly.
Spoon over the strawberries, then dust with icing sugar.

Serves 4

Red Fruit and Custard Filo Parcels

8 large sheets fresh filo pastry,
  cut in half

30g butter, melted, plus extra
  for greasing

55g each of fresh raspberries and
  blackberries (plus extra to decorate)

½ tablespoon soft light brown sugar

4 tablespoons ready-made custard

icing sugar to dust

FRUIT SAUCE

55g each of fresh raspberries and
  blackberries

1 tablespoon caster sugar

1   Preheat the oven to 220°C. Lightly grease a baking sheet. Brush 3 half-sheets of the pastry with the melted butter. Stack them on top of each other, buttered sides up, then place an unbuttered half on top. Repeat with the remaining pastry sheets to make 4 wrappings for the parcels.

2   Mix the raspberries and blackberries with the brown sugar. Spoon 1 tablespoon of custard on top of each pastry stack and brush the edges with butter. Top the custard with a little fruit mixture and gather in the pastry sides, squeezing together to seal. Place on the baking sheet, brush with the remaining butter and cook for 7–10 minutes, until golden.

3   To make the fruit sauce, press the fruit through a sieve and stir in the sugar to taste. Place the parcels on plates and spoon around the sauce. Decorate with the extra raspberries or blackberries and dust with icing sugar.

Serves 4

Note: These little golden parcels have a fabulous range of textures - crisp filo pastry, soft fruit and creamy custard. If you want, you can add a spoonful of plain yoghurt.

Blackcurrant and Lemon Soufflés

170g blackcurrants

100g caster sugar

1 tablespoon Cassis or other fruit liqueur

55g butter, softened, plus extra for greasing

finely grated zest and juice of 1 lemon

3 medium eggs, separated

100g cream cheese

icing sugar to dust

1 Preheat the oven to 190°C. Place the blackcurrants in a small saucepan with ½ the caster sugar and cook for 3 minutes or until they begin to split. Stir in the cassis or other fruit liqueur, then set aside. Lightly grease 4 x 145ml ramekins with butter.

2 Beat the butter with the remaining sugar until pale and creamy. Beat in the lemon zest and juice, egg yolks and cream cheese. Whisk the egg whites until they form stiff peaks (this is best done with an electric whisk). Carefully fold a spoonful of the egg whites into the cream cheese mixture to loosen, then fold in the rest.

3 Divide the blackcurrant mixture between the ramekins and top with the cream cheese mixture. Bake for 30 minutes or until risen and firm. Dust the soufflés with icing sugar and serve immediately.

Serves 4

Note: Hidden under this feather-light lemon soufflé is a layer of juicy blackcurrants. The fruit can get really hot, so make sure you warn everyone not to burn their mouths.

Baked Passion Fruit Custards

4 large eggs, beaten

4 tablespoons caster sugar

145ml coconut milk

pinch of salt

2 passion fruit

1 Preheat the oven to 180°C. Whisk together the eggs, sugar, coconut milk and salt until smooth, then pour into 4 ramekins.

2 Halve 1 passionfruit, scoop out the pulp and seeds and divide between the 4 custard-filled ramekins. Place them in a deep roasting tin.

3 Pour boiling water into the roasting tin to come ¾ of the way up the sides of the ramekins. Bake the custards for 40 minutes. Serve warm or cold with the pulp and seeds from the remaining passion fruit spooned over the top.

Serves 4

Note: This creamy dessert is totally delicious. The passion fruit gives the custard a distinctive sweetness and the seeds add texture, but you can use fresh mango if you prefer.

Cranachan with Raspberries

(see photograph opposite)

30g butter

40g soft dark brown sugar

125g porridge oats

200g ricotta cheese

145ml whipping cream

1–2 tablespoons clear honey, plus extra for trickling (optional)

1–2 tablespoons whisky

250g raspberries

2 tablespoons icing sugar

1 Preheat the oven to 160°C. Melt the butter and sugar in a small saucepan over a low heat, then stir in the oats until well mixed. Turn onto a baking sheet and spread out. Bake for 15 minutes, stirring halfway through, until lightly toasted. Transfer to a plate and leave to cool while you prepare the cream mixture.

2 Beat the ricotta until smooth. Whisk the cream until it forms soft peaks, then fold into the ricotta with 1–2 tablespoons of honey and whisky to taste. Toss the raspberries in the icing sugar.

3 Spoon the ricotta mixture into bowls, top with the oats and finish with the raspberries. Trickle over the extra honey, if desired.

Serves 4

Hazelnut Pancakes with Strawberries

4 medium eggs

½ cup semi-skimmed milk

4 tablespoons clear honey or sugar

100g roasted chopped hazelnuts

100g plain flour

1 teaspoon baking powder

1 teaspoon ground cinnamon

pinch of salt

4 tablespoons butter, melted

SERVE

170ml maple syrup

125g clotted cream

strawberries to garnish

1   Beat the eggs with the milk and honey or sugar until light and fluffy. Gradually add the hazelnuts, flour, baking powder, cinnamon and salt, then beat to a smooth batter.

2   Heat a small, heavy-based frying pan, then brush with ½ teaspoon of the melted butter. Drop in 2 tablespoons of the batter, then quickly tilt the pan to cover the base. Fry for 1–2 minutes, until golden, then turn over and fry for a further minute or until browned. Repeat until all the batter has been used (about 18 pancakes), greasing the pan as necessary.

3   Drizzle the pancakes with maple syrup and serve with clotted cream and strawberries.

Serves 6

Note: These nutty pancakes are so delicious, you just have to eat them as soon as they're ready. If you can't get hold of strawberries, try them with sliced bananas.

Red Berry and Banana Pie

12 pecan nuts, roughly chopped

340g plain flour, sifted

1½ teaspoons baking powder

200g chilled butter, cubed, plus extra
  for greasing

4 ripe bananas

4 tablespoons demerara sugar

125g raspberries

4 tablespoons redcurrants or
  blackcurrants

1 Finely grind the nuts in a food processor, or use a pestle and mortar. Put 1 tablespoon of the ground nuts and all the flour into a bowl, then rub in the butter with your fingertips, until the mixture resembles fine breadcrumbs.

2 Remove and reserve ¼ of the mixture for the topping. Add 4–5 tablespoons of cold water to the remaining mixture and mix to a firm dough. Cover and refrigerate for 30 minutes.

3 Preheat the oven to 190°C. Grease a 20cm spring-form tin. Roll out the pastry on a lightly floured surface, then use it to line the tin. Line the pastry with baking paper and fill with baking beans. Bake for 15 minutes. Remove the paper and beans. Bake for 5 minutes until golden.

4 Slice the bananas into a bowl, stir in ½ the sugar, then fold in the rest of the fruit. Spoon into the pastry case. Mix the reserved flour mixture with the rest of the sugar and the ground nuts and sprinkle over the fruit. Bake for 15 minutes, then reduce the oven temperature to 180°C and bake for a further 15–20 minutes, until the top is golden. Cool for a few minutes before serving.

Serves 6

Note: The crunchy crumble topping and nutty rich pastry make a perfect contrast to the soft berries and bananas. A spoonful of creamy plain yoghurt makes it even better.

Pear, Raspberry and Almond Sponge

⅘ cup dry or slightly sweet white wine

2–3 strips lemon zest, pared with a vegetable peeler, and juice of 1 lemon

2 tablespoons clear honey or sugar

4 whole cloves

4 large ripe pears, peeled, quartered and cored

100g butter, softened

55g caster sugar

grated zest of ½ orange

3 eggs, lightly beaten

145g ground almonds

2 teaspoons orange-flower water or vanilla extract (optional)

125g fresh raspberries

sifted icing sugar to dust

1   Preheat the oven to 180°C. Place the wine, lemon zest and juice, honey or sugar and cloves in a saucepan. Bring to the boil, then simmer, uncovered, for 5 minutes or until reduced slightly. Add the pears, cover and cook for 5 minutes or until tender. Transfer the pears to a dish, drain and cool. Strain the cooking liquid, discarding the lemon zest and cloves, and reserve.

2   Beat the butter, caster sugar and orange zest until light and fluffy (this is easiest with an electric whisk). Gradually add the eggs, almonds, orange-flower water or vanilla extract (if using) and beat until smooth.

3   Arrange the pears in a 25cm flan dish. Sprinkle over ½ the raspberries and top with the egg mixture, smoothing with the back of a spoon. Bake for 25–30 minutes, until firm to the touch.

4   Meanwhile, put the reserved liquid into a small saucepan and bring to the boil. Boil for 5 minutes or until reduced to about 3 tablespoons. Increase the oven temperature to 230°C. Spoon the liquid over the flan and bake for 5 minutes longer or until golden. Cool slightly, then decorate with the remaining raspberries and dust with icing sugar.

Serves 6

Note: This is irresistible with clotted cream. It also works with canned pears, which don't need cooking. Swap the syrup for the poaching liquid.

Brazil Nut Shortbreads with Strawberries

SHORTBREAD

30g Brazil nuts

55g brown sugar

125g plain flour

75g butter, softened

2 medium egg yolks

FILLING

1 teaspoon grated orange zest, plus
extra to decorate

250g extra thick cream

250g strawberries, hulled and sliced

4 tablespoons strawberry jam

1 Place the nuts and sugar in a food processor and blend until fine. Add the flour and butter and blend until the mixture resembles fine breadcrumbs. Add the egg yolks and pulse until the mixture forms a soft dough (taking care not to over-process.) Bring the mixture together to form a ball, then wrap in plastic wrap and chill for 20 minutes.

2 Preheat the oven to 180°C. On a lightly floured surface, roll out the dough to ½cm thick and stamp out 8 x 7½cm rounds with a biscuit cutter, re-rolling as necessary. Place on a greased baking tray and bake for 10–12 minutes, until lightly golden. Cool on a wire rack.

3 To make the filling, fold the orange zest into the cream. Place a small amount of cream on a biscuit, top with strawberries, then another biscuit, then more cream and strawberries. Warm the jam in a small saucepan, then drizzle it over the top. Decorate with orange zest. Repeat with the remaining biscuits.

Serves 4

Note: Fresh strawberries are sandwiched with cream between melt-in-the-mouth biscuits and served with a drizzle of strawberry jelly – simply delicious. Strawberries contain more vitamin C than any other berry and a typical portion contains only 28 calories. Brazil nuts are rich in selenium, a powerful antioxidant needed for fertility, and healthy skin and hair.

winter
favorites

Lemon and Cinnamon Eve's Pudding

(see photograph on page 44)

500g cooking apples, peeled, cored and chopped

100g caster sugar

½ teaspoon ground cinnamon

100g soft margarine

finely grated rind of 1 lemon and juice of ½ lemon

2 medium eggs, lightly beaten

100g plain flour, sifted with ½ teaspoon baking powder

1 Preheat the oven to 180°C. Place the apples in a saucepan with 2 tablespoons of the sugar and 1 tablespoon of water. Cover and cook over a low heat for 3–4 minutes, until the apples begin to soften, then add the cinnamon and stir. Transfer to a 23 x 15cm oven-proof dish.

2 Beat the margarine and the remaining sugar until pale and creamy, then add the lemon rind and juice, the eggs and flour mixture. Beat the mixture to a soft, dropping consistency.

3 Spoon the mixture over the apples, smooth with the back of a spoon, and bake for 25–30 minutes, until well risen, golden and just firm to the touch.

Serves 4

Note: The old-fashioned recipes are often the best. In this comforting pudding, a lemony sponge covers cinnamon-scented apples. Cream goes with it perfectly.

Blueberry and Orange Clafoutis

(see photograph opposite)

2 tablespoons butter, melted plus extra for greasing

200g blueberries

3 medium eggs

75g caster sugar

few drops vanilla extract

finely grated zest and juice of ½ orange

55g plain flour, sifted

145g sour cream

icing sugar to dust

1 Preheat the oven to 190°C. Grease a shallow 20cm ovenproof dish with butter, then spoon in the blueberries.

2 Place the eggs, caster sugar, vanilla extract, orange zest and juice and the flour in a bowl, then beat until smooth. Gently stir in the sour cream and melted butter, then pour the mixture over the blueberries. Bake for 40 minutes or until risen and set. Cool for 5 minutes, then dust with icing sugar.

Serves 4

Note: This light batter pudding is much easier to make than it looks. You can use many other fruits instead of blueberries, but dark red cherries are particularly good.

Date Puddings with Sticky Toffee Sauce

75g butter, softened, plus extra for greasing

100g stoned dates, chopped

100g soft light brown sugar

½ teaspoon vanilla extract

2 large eggs

100g wholemeal flour

1½ teaspoons baking powder

1 very ripe banana, mashed

TOFFEE SAUCE

85g soft dark brown sugar

55g butter

2 tablespoons light cream

1 Preheat the oven to 180°C. Grease 4 x 200ml pudding basins or ramekins with butter. Cover the dates with boiling water and soak for 10 minutes to soften.

2 Beat the butter, light brown sugar and vanilla extract until pale and creamy. Beat in the eggs, then fold in the flour and baking powder. Strain the dates and blend to a purée in a food processor or mash with a fork. Then stir into the mixture with the banana.

3 Spoon the mixture into the basins or ramekins, almost to their tops, and place on a baking sheet. Bake for 20 minutes or until risen and just firm to the touch. Cool for 5 minutes, then loosen the puddings with a knife and invert onto plates.

4 To make the sauce, place the dark brown sugar, butter and cream in a pan and heat gently for 5 minutes or until syrupy. Pour over the puddings to serve.

Serves 4

Note: Sponge pudding, bananas, dates and a sticky toffee sauce – what a combination! You can serve it on its own or with a big scoop of good vanilla ice cream.

Indian Rice Pudding with Pistachios

55g basmati rice

1⅗ cups whole milk

400ml evaporated milk

butter for greasing

3 cardamom pods, husks discarded and seeds reserved

1 cinnamon stick

55g caster sugar

2 tablespoons roasted flaked almonds

30g shelled pistachios, roughly chopped

1 Preheat the oven to 150°C. Place the rice, milk and evaporated milk in a small, heavy-based saucepan and bring to a simmer, taking care not to let the mixture boil. Simmer, uncovered, for 10 minutes.

2 Butter an ovenproof dish. Transfer the rice mixture to the dish, then stir in the cardamom seeds, cinnamon, sugar, and nuts, reserving 1 tablespoon of pistachios to garnish. Bake for 2 hours, or until reduced to a thick consistency, stirring in the skin that forms on top every 30 minutes. Remove the cinnamon stick. Serve warm or cold, garnished with the reserved pistachios.

Serves 4

Note: Even those put off by the British version of rice pudding will like this variation. Flavoured with spices and nuts, it's a great way to end an Indian meal.

Plum Tart with Crumble Topping

200g unsweetened shortcrust pastry,
  defrosted
  if frozen

400g plums or damsons, halved
  and stoned

3 tablespoons caster sugar

1 teaspoon cornflour

55g chopped mixed nuts

2 tablespoons demerara sugar

2 tablespoons fresh breadcrumbs

1   Preheat the oven to 190°C. Roll the pastry out thinly on a lightly floured surface and line an 20cm loose-bottomed flan tin. Refrigerate for 10 minutes, then line with baking paper and baking beans. Bake for 15 minutes, then remove the paper and beans and bake for another 5 minutes or until lightly golden. Cool for 5 minutes.

2   Meanwhile, put the plums or damsons into a saucepan with 4 tablespoons of water and the caster sugar. Cook gently, covered, for 5 minutes or until the fruit is soft. Blend the cornflour with 1 tablespoon of water. Stir into the fruit mixture and cook for 1 minute or until the juices thicken slightly.

3   Place the plums or damsons cut-side up, with any juices in the pastry case. Mix together the nuts, raw sugar and breadcrumbs and sprinkle over the fruit. Bake for 15 minutes or until the topping is golden.

Serves 6

Note: Served hot with lashings of custard, this pudding is perfect for a cold winter's night. You can make it a day in advance and reheat it, but keep it in the fridge.

Pear and Almond Flan

2 large, firm pears, peeled, cored and sliced

1 teaspoon lemon juice

55g caster sugar

200g unsweetened shortcrust pastry, defrosted if frozen

3–4 tablespoons apricot or plum jam

55g soft margarine

1 medium egg

55g plain flour

1/4 teaspoon baking powder

55g ground almonds

30g flaked almonds

icing sugar to dust

1 Preheat the oven 180°C. Toss the pears with the lemon juice and 1 teaspoon of the caster sugar.

2 Roll the pastry out thinly on a lightly floured surface and line an 20cm loosebottomed flan tin. Refrigerate for 10 minutes. Line the pastry with baking paper and a layer of baking beans and cook for 15 minutes. Remove the paper and beans and bake for another 5 minutes or until lightly golden. Leave to cool for 5 minutes.

3 Spread the jam over the pastry and top with the pears. Beat the margarine and remaining sugar until pale and creamy, then add the egg, flour and ground almonds and beat to a soft, dropping consistency. Spoon the mixture over the pears, sprinkle with the flaked almonds and cook for 30 minutes or until set and golden. Cool for 10 minutes, then transfer to a plate and dust with icing sugar.

Serves 6

Note: Hidden in the middle of this sophisticated pudding is a layer of jam, which makes it sweeter and even more delicious. Serve with a little cream or crème fraîche.

Ginger and Pear Steamed Pudding

145 butter, softened, plus extra for greasing

145g light muscovado sugar, plus 1 tablespoon to coat

3 ripe pears, peeled and cored, 1 chopped, 2 sliced

3 pieces preserved ginger, chopped, and 5 tablespoons syrup

2 large eggs, beaten

170g plain flour

½ teaspoon baking powder

2 teaspoons ground ginger

30g fresh white breadcrumbs

finely grated zest of 1 lemon

1 Grease a 1.2 litre pudding basin with butter and coat with 1 tablespoon of sugar. Carefully line the base and sides of the basin with the pear slices, then drizzle over ½ the ginger syrup.

2 Beat together the butter and sugar until light and fluffy, then gradually beat in the eggs. Sift together the flour and ground ginger, then fold into the butter mixture. Stir in the breadcrumbs, lemon zest, remaining syrup, the preserved ginger and the chopped pear. Spoon into the basin and level the top, then cover the basin with a double layer each of baking paper and foil. Tie a piece of string around the rim of the basin to hold the layers in place, then cut off any excess paper and foil.

3 Place the basin in a saucepan and pour in boiling water to reach halfway up the basin. Bring back to the boil, then simmer, covered, for 1½ hours, adding more water as necessary. Remove the basin from the water and leave to cool for 5 minutes. Invert onto a plate, tap the base and remove the basin.

Serves 4

Note: The ginger and pear flavours mingle beautifully in this surprisingly light pudding. Serve with lots of custard.

Caramelised Rice Pudding with Apricots

75g pudding rice

200g caster sugar

2 vanilla pods, 1 split in half
lengthways

30g unsalted butter

2⅖ cups whole milk

145g double cream

2 strips lemon zest and juice of 1 lemon

250g dried apricots

1–2 tablespoons orange liqueur,
such as Cointreau

1 Put the rice into a saucepan, cover with water and boil for 5 minutes. Drain. Return the rice to the pan with 40g of the sugar, the split vanilla pod, the butter and the milk. Simmer for 45–60 minutes, stirring often, until thickened. Transfer to a bowl and cool for 20 minutes. Remove the vanilla pod and scrape the seeds into the rice. Discard the pod. Whisk the cream until it forms soft peaks, then fold into the rice.

2 Meanwhile, put 100g of the sugar into a saucepan with the lemon zest, the remaining vanilla pod and 4/5 cup of water. Heat, stirring, for 3 minutes or until the sugar dissolves. Add the apricots and cook for 20 minutes to reduce the syrup.

3 Put the apricots into 4 ramekins, add the lemon juice, liqueur and syrup, then cool for 5 minutes. Top with the rice pudding, then refrigerate for 1 hour. Preheat the grill to high. Sprinkle the puddings with the rest of the sugar. Grill for 1–2 minutes, until the sugar caramelises, then cool for a few minutes.

Serves 4

Note: You'll forget any schoolday horrors of stodgy rice pudding when you taste this apricot version topped with caramel.

Golden Oaty Apple Pudding

145g butter, plus extra for greasing

680g cooking apples, peeled, cored and chopped

200g dried apricots, chopped

2 tablespoons raisins

55g sugar

4 tablespoons golden syrup

1–2 teaspoons finely grated fresh root ginger

250g rolled oats

1 Preheat the oven to 190°C. Butter a 20cm shallow ovenproof dish.

2 Place the apples, apricots, raisins, half the sugar and 1–2 tablespoons of water in a saucepan. Cover the pan, then cook over a low heat for 10–15 minutes, stirring occasionally until the apples soften, then set aside.

3 Heat the remaining sugar with the butter, golden syrup and ginger in a saucepan for 1–2 minutes, until the sugar dissolves, then stir in the oats. Add ¾ of the mixture to the dish, using a wooden spoon to spread it evenly over the base and sides. Smooth the fruit mixture on top, then spoon over the remaining oat mixture and press down lightly with the back of the spoon. Cook for 30 minutes or until the top is golden.

Serves 4

Note: Fresh root ginger gives this apple pudding a deeper and more pungent taste than its ground equivalent and it complements the fruity filling perfectly.

Citrus Bread and Butter Pudding

35g butter, softened, plus extra
   for greasing

finely grated zest of 1 lemon finely
   grated zest and juice of 1 orange

6 slices white sliced bread,
   crusts removed

55g raisins

1 cup extra thick cream, plus extra to
   serve (optional)

4 medium egg yolks

85g brown sugar

1 In a small bowl, mix together the butter, lemon and orange zest and orange juice. Spread the bread with the flavoured butter and cut each slice into 4 triangles. Sprinkle the raisins over the base of a 1 litre greased, shallow, ovenproof dish and arrange the bread on top.

2 Gently heat the cream, and bring it just to the boil. In a bowl, whisk the egg yolks with the sugar, until just pale. Pour the cream in and stir well. Pour the mixture over the bread and leave to stand for 20 minutes, to allow the bread to soak up the liquid.

3 Preheat the oven to 180°C. Place the pudding dish in a large roasting tin. Pour boiling water into the tin to come halfway up the sides of the dish. Bake for 30 minutes, until crisp and golden on top and lightly set. Serve with extra thick cream (if using), or just on its own.

Serves 4

Note: This traditional nursery pudding is given a fresh twist with lively, citrus flavours White bread, though not thought to be as good as wholemeal bread, is still a good source of fibre and by law it has to be fortified with calcium and B vitamins. Citrus fruits are an excellent source of vitamin C.

Apple Dumplings with Butterscotch

500g fresh puff or unsweetened
  shortcrust pastry

30g shelled pecans, chopped

30g stoned dates, finely chopped

½ teaspoon ground cinnamon

6 apples, peeled

1 small egg yolk, beaten with

2 tablespoons milk

SAUCE

85g butter

145g light muscovado sugar

145ml double cream

lemon juice

1   To make the sauce, place the butter, sugar and cream in a heavy-based saucepan and stir until the butter melts. Boil for 2–3 minutes, until thickened, then add the lemon juice to taste. Set aside.

2   Roll out the pastry on a lightly floured surface and cut out 6 circles just large enough to enclose the apples. Cut some leaves from trimmings for decoration. Place the circles on a baking sheet.

3   Combine the pecans, dates and cinnamon with 6 tablespoons of the sauce. Cut out the centre of each apple to remove the core. Put an apple on each pastry circle, then half-fill it with the pecan mixture. Gather up the pastry, brush the edges with the egg yolk mixture and pinch together, then brush all over with the egg yolk mixture and decorate with the reserved pastry leaves. Refrigerate for 1 hour.

4   Preheat the oven to 190°C. Bake for 35–45 minutes, until the pastry is golden and the apples are tender. Gently reheat the remaining sauce and serve with the apples.

Serves 6

Note: Hidden inside these pastry-covered apples is a wonderful mixture of crunchy pecan nuts and cinnamon-spiced dates.

Date and Walnut Baklava

250g dried stoned dates, chopped

finely grated zest and juice of 1 orange

125g walnut pieces, chopped

½ teaspoon ground cinnamon

75g butter, melted

12 sheets fresh filo pastry, trimmed to fit the tin

1 teaspoon sesame seeds

145g clear honey

juice of ½ lemon

1 Preheat the oven to 180°C. Simmer the dates and orange juice in a saucepan for 4–5 minutes, until the liquid is just absorbed. Stir in the zest, walnuts and cinnamon. Brush a shallow 20cm square tin with butter. Keeping the remaining pastry covered, lay 1 sheet in the tin and brush with butter. Top with another sheet and brush again. Repeat to form 8 layers in total.

2 Spread ½ the date mixture over the pastry and top with 2 buttered sheets. Spread with the remaining filling and finish with 2 more buttered sheets. Tuck in the edges, score a diamond pattern on top and sprinkle with the sesame seeds. Bake for 30 minutes or until golden, then reduce the oven to 150°C and bake for 30–40 minutes.

3 Simmer the honey, lemon juice and 200ml of water in a pan for 10–15 minutes, until reduced by ½, then leave to cool for 20 minutes. Pour over the baklava and cool for 1 hour before slicing.

Serves 6

Note: A delicious filling of nuts, moist fruit and spices oozes out of this sweet, gooey Turkish treat.

Upside-Down Apple Tart

100g plain flour

1 tablespoon cornflour

pinch of salt

1 tablespoon icing sugar

145g unsalted butter, softened

55g soft light brown sugar

pinch of ground cinnamon

2 cooking apples or 4 eating apples,
   peeled, cored and sliced

1 Preheat the oven to 180°C. Sift the flour with the cornflour, salt and icing sugar, then mix in 100g of the butter until the mixture forms a soft ball. Shape into a round, wrap in plastic wrap and refrigerate for 10 minutes.

2 Place the brown sugar, the remaining butter and the cinnamon in an ovenproof frying pan or 20cm shallow non-stick cake tin. Heat in the oven for 3 minutes or until the sugar turns syrupy.

3 Arrange the apples in the tin. Roll out the pastry between 2 sheets of baking paper until it is just larger than the pan or tin. Place the pastry on top of the apples, tucking the edge into the inside of the pan or tin. Bake for 35–40 minutes, until the pastry is crisp and golden. Cool for 10 minutes, then invert onto a serving plate.

Serves 6

Note: This twist on a traditional French apple tart (tarte tatin), uses a delicious shortbread-style pastry. If you're in a hurry, use a sheet of ready-made puff pastry instead.

Extra-light Banana Clafoutis

75g butter, melted

4 tablespoons molasses or soft dark
  brown sugar

grated zest and juice of 1 lemon

4 tablespoons rum

1 kg bananas, cut into chunks

1 cup semi-skimmed milk

4 eggs, separated

3 tablespoons sugar

100g plain flour

1 teaspoon ground cinnamon

icing sugar to dust

1 Preheat the oven to 220°C. Place the butter, molasses or brown sugar, lemon
zest, juice and rum in a 33 x 23cm ovenproof dish and mix well. Add the
bananas and toss to coat. Cook for 12–15 minutes, basting frequently, until
the bananas have softened.

2 Meanwhile, gently warm the milk in a small saucepan. Beat the egg yolks
and sugar until pale and creamy. Beat in the warmed milk, then the flour and
cinnamon. Whisk the whites until they form soft peaks, then fold gently into
the mixture.

3 Remove the bananas from the oven and reduce the temperature to 200°C.
Pour the batter over the bananas and return the dish to the oven. Bake for
20–25 minutes, until browned and well-risen. Check the pudding is cooked
by inserting a skewer into the centre; it should come out clean. Allow to cool
slightly – the mixture will sink rapidly as it cools – then dust with icing sugar
and serve warm.

Serves 6

*Note: Clafoutis is traditionally made with cherries, but using bananas gives
the pudding a wonderful richness. It's good served on its own, with double
cream or vanilla ice cream.*

Pecan and Orange Tart

200g shortcrust pastry, defrosted
   if frozen

1 large egg

5 tablespoon maple syrup or clear
   honey

pinch of salt

1 teaspoon finely grated orange zest

55g caster sugar

55g butter, melted

125g pecan nuts

1 Preheat the oven to 200°C. Roll the pastry out thinly on a lightly floured surface and use it to line an 20cm loose-bottomed flan tin. Refrigerate for 10 minutes.

2 Line the pastry with baking paper and baking beans. Cook for 15 minutes, then remove the paper and beans and cook for another 5 minutes or until lightly golden. Cool for 5 minutes.

3 Whisk the egg with the maple syrup or honey, salt, orange zest, sugar and butter until blended. Pour the mixture into the pastry case and arrange the pecan nuts on top. Bake for 30 minutes or until set. Cool in the tin for 15 minutes.

Serves 6

Note: This fabulous version of pecan pie is very easy to make. It's irresistible when served warm from the oven with vanilla ice cream or clotted cream.

Quick Apple Strudel

6 sheets filo pastry

½ cup soft breadcrumbs

2 x 415g cans apple pieces

½ cup sultanas

½ teaspoon ground cloves

½ teaspoon mixed spice

1 tablespoon melted butter

1 teaspoon icing sugar

1   Lay pastry sheets under a damp tea-towel, sprinkling breadcrumbs between each sheet.

2   Mix apple, sultanas, cloves and mixed spice together. Spread apple mixture down centre of pastry to within 3cm of ends.

3   Roll one long end of pastry layer over filling and roll as for a sponge roll. Place on a baking tray.

4   Mix melted butter and icing sugar together. Brush around edges of pastry. Fold in short ends over filling. Roll from long side as for a sponge roll.

5   Place on a baking tray. Brush with remaining butter mixture. Slash strudel top. Bake at 200°C for 20 to 25 minutes or until pastry is lightly golden and cooked. Serve warm.

Serves 8–10

Tropical Clafouti

250g pot cream cheese

3 eggs

½ cup sugar

½ cup custard powder

432g can pineapple chunks in natural juice

2 teaspoons grated lemon rind

¼ cup passion fruit pulp

¼ cup desiccated coconut

1 Soften cream cheese and place in the bowl of a food processor or blender with eggs, sugar, custard powder, crushed pineapple and lemon rind. Process or blend until well combined.

2 Add passion fruit pulp and mix in quickly so as not to crush seeds. Pour into a greased 20cm quiche dish. Sprinkle over coconut.

3 Bake at 180°C for 30 to 40 minutes or until set. Serve warm.

Serves 6–8

Gullible Pudding

415g can apple pieces

1 cup flour

1 teaspoon baking powder

½ cup rolled oats

100g butter

½ cup brown sugar

1 tablespoon cornflour

¼ cup boiling water

1 Place apple in an ovenproof dish.

2 Mix flour, baking powder and rolled oats together. Melt butter and mix through flour mixture. Sprinkle over apple.

3 Mix brown sugar and cornflour together. Sprinkle over flour mixture. Pour boiling water over the back of a spoon onto the pudding.

4 Bake at 180°C for 25 minutes or until crusty on top. Serve hot with custard.

Serves 4

Strawberry Shortcake

1½ cups flour

1 teaspoon baking powder

¼ cup icing sugar

150g butter

1 egg

250g cream cheese

¼ cup icing sugar

½ cup strawberry jam

2 cups strawberries

½ cup sugar

½ cup water

1 Place flour, baking powder and icing sugar in the bowl of a food processor or a bowl. Mix to combine. Cut in butter until mixture resembles fine crumbs. Add egg and a little water if necessary to make a stiff dough.

2 Make a 20cm circle on a baking-paper-covered oven tray. Press dough out to fill the circle.

3 Bake at 190°C for 20 to 25 minutes. Cool.

4 Soften cream cheese and mix in icing sugar. Spread shortcake with cream cheese then spread over jam. Hull strawberries and cut in half if large. Arrange strawberries over shortcake.

5 Heat sugar and water together over a medium heat, stirring until dissolved. Increase heat and cook sugar mixture until a light golden. Remove from heat. Cool slightly then pour over strawberries. Working quickly, use a fork to pull threads up from the caramel.

Serves 4–6

Note: You can use this idea with virtually any berries, matching the jam to suit. Try a mixture of berries for a good look. It sure beats that boring bowl of strawberries we see served au natural every summer.

Opera House Tart with Ruby Sauce

PASTRY

1 cup polenta

½ cup cornflour

½ cup flour

½ cup sugar

150g butter

1 egg

1 tablespoon raw sugar

FILLING

2 x 415g cans pear halves in light
  syrup

1½ cups red wine

¾ cup sugar

1 cinnamon stick

5cm piece lemon rind

4 whole cloves

1 Place polenta, cornflour, flour and sugar in the bowl of a food processor or bowl. Mix to combine. Add butter and mix or rub in until mixture resembles coarse crumbs. Mix in egg to make a stiff dough.

2 Refrigerate while preparing filling. Cut dough in half and press dough into the base of a 20cm round loose-bottom cake tin.

3 Press or lightly roll second half to a 20cm circle. Place cooked drained pears on pastry. Top with pastry circle. Sprinkle over raw sugar.

4 Bake at 200°C for 25 minutes or until pastry is lightly golden and cooked. Serve hot with wine sauce and cream.

FILLING

1 Drain pears. Mix pear juice, wine, sugar, cinnamon stick, lemon rind and cloves together in a saucepan. Bring to the boil. Add pears and simmer for 5 minutes.

2 Drain pears from wine mixture and set aside to cool. Bring wine mixture back to the boil and heat for 8 minutes or until sauce is reduced by half. Serve warm.

Serves 4–6

Pear Tart Tatin with Ginger Cream

415g can pear halves in natural juice

50g butter

1 cup sugar

½ teaspoon ground ginger

2 sheets flaky puff pastry

1 tablespoon melted butter

GINGER CREAM

300ml cream

2 teaspoons icing sugar

1 teaspoon grated lemon rind

2 tablespoons reserved pear juice

1 teaspoon ground ginger

1 Drain pears, reserving juice. Cut pear halves into thin slices. Melt butter and sugar in a large frying pan with a metal handle. Heat until bubbling. Arrange pears, cartwheel fashion, in the butter mixture. Sprinkle over ginger.

2 Brush one pastry sheet with melted butter and place second sheet on top. Cut pastry to fit the diameter of the frying pan. Place pastry on top of pears and cook on top of stove over a medium heat for 15 minutes.

3 Remove pan from stove and place in a 200°C oven for 10 minutes or until pastry is golden. Remove from oven and turn tatin onto a serving plate. Serve hot with Ginger Cream.

GINGER CREAM

1 Whip cream until soft. Mix in icing sugar, lemon rind, pear juice and ginger until combined and the preferred consistency.

Serves 4–6

dessert cakes

Over-The-Top Dessert Cake

(see photograph on page 74)

3 egg whites

¾ cup sugar

½ cup toasted ground hazelnuts

whipped cream

prepared caramel sauce

prepared chocolate sauce

fresh or canned fruit

1 Beat egg whites until stiff. Beat in sugar until mixture is thick and glossy. Fold in hazelnuts.

2 Mark two 20cm circles on a piece of baking paper. Spread mixture out to an 18cm circle.

3 Bake at 150°C for 50 minutes to 1 hour or until meringue is dry and crisp. Cool in oven.

4 To serve, fill and top with whipped cream. Drizzle over caramel and chocolate sauces and garnish with fresh seasonal fruit, drained canned fruit or a mixture of both.

Serves 6–8

Note: This is a sugar fix cake that will make every sweet tooth fizz out. It is superbly decadent! We use bought sauces for this.

Mocha Dessert Cake

(see photograph on opposite page)

100g cooking chocolate

150g butter

1 cup sugar

1 cup strong black coffee

1 cup flour

¼ cup cornflour

1 egg

cocoa

1 Mix chocolate, butter, sugar and coffee in a saucepan large enough to mix all the ingredients and heat gently until butter and chocolate have melted and mixture is smooth. Remove from heat.

2 Sift in flour and cornflour and add egg. Beat with a wooden spoon until smooth. Baking-paper-line the bottom of a 20cm round cake tin and pour mixture into tin.

3 Bake at 160°C for 50 to 60 minutes or until cake is firm. Stand in tin for 10 minutes before turning onto a cooling rack. Serve dusted with cocoa and accompanied with fruit.

Serves 6–8

Fig and Roasted Almond Cake

(see photograph opposite, top)

1 cup chopped figs

½ cup boiling water

1 cup roasted almonds

4 egg whites

½ cup brown sugar

1 tablespoon icing sugar

½ teaspoon cinnamon

SPICED CREAM

300ml cream

1 teaspoon cinnamon

1 Cook figs in boiling water for 10 minutes. Cool. Mix in almonds. Beat egg whites and brown sugar together until stiff peaks form. Fold figs and almonds into meringue.

2 Spread into a 20cm round baking-paper-lined loose-bottom cake tin. Bake at 180°C for 45 minutes or until lightly golden and set. Cool for 10 minutes before removing from tin.

3 When ready to serve, mix icing sugar and cinnamon together. Sprinkle over cake. Serve with spiced cream.

SPICED CREAM

1 Beat cream and cinnamon until soft peaks form.

Serves 6–8

Note: Roast almonds at 180°C for 7 to 10 minutes. Roasted or toasted nuts have much better flavour and texture in any dish.

Espresso Cake

(see photograph opposite, bottom)

1 cup boiling water

¼ cup ground espresso coffee beans

200g butter

1¼ cups sugar

3 eggs

1 tablespoon vanilla essence

2 cups flour

3 teaspoons baking powder

¼ cup finely ground espresso coffee beans

8 sugar cubes

cinnamon

COFFEE FLAVOURED CREAM

300ml cream

1 tablespoon icing sugar

2 tablespoons very strong espresso coffee

1 Pour boiling water over first measure of ground coffee and leave to steep for 5 minutes. Strain liquid from beans and pour over butter in a large bowl, stirring until butter melts. Mix in sugar, eggs and vanilla and beat with a wooden spoon until combined. Sift flour and baking powder into mixture and mix in with second measure of coffee.

2 Pour the mixture into a baking-paper-lined 20cm square cake tin. Bake at 180°C for 50 to 55 minutes or until cake springs back when lightly touched.

3 Crush sugar cubes. Sprinkle over hot cake. Cool in tin for 10 minutes before turning onto a cooling rack. Dust with cinnamon and serve with coffee flavoured cream.

COFFEE FLAVOURED CREAM

1 Whip cream until soft. Beat in icing sugar and coffee.

Serves 8–10

Apricot Cake

2 x 415g cans apricot halves in natural juice

125g butter

1 cup sugar

2 eggs

2 cups flour

4 teaspoons baking powder

TOPPING

¼ cup flour

¼ cup rolled oats

2 tablespoons brown sugar

1 teaspoon baking powder

50g butter

1 Purée one can of apricots and juice in a food processor or blender. Drain second tin of apricots.

2 Melt butter in a saucepan large enough to mix all the ingredients. Stir in sugar and beat in eggs, flour, baking powder and apricot purée with a wooden spoon.

3 Pour into a baking-paper-lined 20cm round deep cake tin. Arrange drained apricots over surface of cake. Sprinkle with topping.

4 Bake at 180°C for 1 hour or until an inserted skewer comes out clean. Serve warm with whipped cream.

TOPPING

1 Mix flour, rolled oats, brown sugar and baking powder together. Rub in butter until mixture resembles coarse crumbs.

Serves 8–10

Lemon Semolina Cake

125g butter

1 cup sugar

3 eggs

2 teaspoons grated lemon rind

½ cup semolina

1 cup flour

2 teaspoons baking powder

¼ cup lemon juice

¼ cup icing sugar

1 Melt butter in a saucepan large enough to mix all the ingredients. Remove from heat and mix in sugar. Add eggs, lemon rind and semolina. Beat until well combined. Sift flour and baking powder into mixture and mix thoroughly.

2 Pour into a baking-paper-lined 20cm round cake tin. Bake at 180°C for 35 minutes.

3 Mix lemon juice and icing sugar together. Remove cake from oven and pour over lemon juice mixture.

4 Return to oven and bake for a further 10 minutes. Serve warm or at room temperature with lemon flavoured yogurt.

Serves 6–8

Note: Semolina is usually found in the supermarket bulk bins or in packets in the cereal or baking section of the supermarket.

Harlequin Brownies

250g cream cheese

½ cup sugar

2 eggs

1 teaspoon vanilla essence

200g butter

¼ cup cocoa

1 cup sugar

2 eggs

¾ cup flour

1 teaspoon baking powder

1 Soften cream cheese and mix with sugar, eggs and vanilla until smooth. Set aside. Melt butter in a large saucepan. Mix in cocoa. Remove from heat and add sugar and eggs. Beat until smooth. Sift in flour and baking powder. Mix until smooth.

2 Pour half the chocolate mixture into a baking-paper-lined 20 x 30cm sponge roll tin. Arrange dollops of cream cheese mixture over the top of chocolate mixture. Pour over remaining chocolate mixture. Swirl a knife through the mixtures to marble the brownie.

3 Bake at 180°C for 30 minutes or until brownie springs back when lightly touched. Serve with fruit and chocolate sauce.

Serves 8–10

Ruth's Rum and Raisin Torte

1 cup raisins

2 tablespoons rum

1 cup chopped walnuts

3 egg whites

½ cup caster sugar

icing sugar

1 Heat raisins and rum together until boiling. Remove from heat and set aside to cool while preparing remaining ingredients.

2 Mix in walnuts. Beat egg whites until stiff. Gradually beat in sugar, beating until stiff, glossy meringue forms. Fold raisin mixture in.

3 Spread in a 20cm round baking-paper-lined sponge tin. Bake at 160°C for 45 minutes or until firm to the touch. Cool in tin.

4 When cold dust with icing sugar. Serve cut into wedges.

Serves 6

Baked Cherry Cheesecake

(see photograph opposite, bottom)

250g packet chocolate chip biscuits

75g butter

FILLING

250g cream cheese

¼ cup cream

1 egg

1 egg yolk

¼ cup sugar

425g can pitted cherries

1 teaspoon almond essence

1 Crush biscuits until fine crumbs. Melt butter. Mix crumbs and butter together and line the base and sides of a 20cm round springform tin with the crumb mixture.

2 Bake at 160°C for 10 minutes or until firm.

3 Pour in filling and bake at 160°C for 40 minutes or until filling is set.

4 Serve with sweetened sour cream and fresh cherries if available.

FILLING

1 Soften cream cheese. Gradually beat in cream. Beat egg, egg yolk and sugar together. Mix into cream cheese mixture with cherries and almond essence.

Serves 6–8

Chilled Tropical Cheesecake

(see photograph opposite, top)

125g coconut biscuits

50g butter

2 passion fruit

FILLING

440g can pineapple chunks

1 tablespoon gelatin

250g cream cheese

250g cottage cheese

½ cup coconut cream

¼ cup sugar

¼ cup passion fruit pulp

1½ cups cream

1 Crush biscuits until fine crumbs. Melt butter and mix into biscuit crumbs. Press into the base of a 20cm round springform tin.

2 Refrigerate while preparing filling. Pour filling into tin and refrigerate until set.

3 Decorate with remaining cream and pulp from passion fruit.

FILLING

1 Drain pineapple, reserving 1 cup of juice. Pour juice into a saucepan. Sprinkle over gelatin and leave for 5 minutes to soften and swell. Heat until gelatin has dissolved.

2 Cool then refrigerate until the consistency of raw egg white.

3 Place the pineapple chunks in a blender or food processor to create pineapple pulp.

4 Soften cream cheese and beat with cottage cheese, coconut cream and sugar until creamy. Mix in partially set pineapple juice, pineapple pulp and passion fruit pulp. Beat cream until soft peaks form. Fold half of the cream into the pineapple mixture.

Serves 6–8

Apple Cream Cheesecake

8 coconut biscuits

250g cream cheese

3 eggs

¾ cup sugar

1 cup cream

415g can apple pieces

2 teaspoons grated lemon rind

2 tablespoons gelatin

½ cup sweet white wine

apple slices

desiccated coconut, toasted

1 Place a biscuit in the base of eight baking-paper-lined half-cup capacity ramekins. Soften cream cheese and beat with eggs and sugar until smooth. Whip cream until soft peaks form. Fold into cream cheese mixture with apple and lemon rind.

2 Soften gelatin in wine. Stand over hot water until gelatin dissolves. Mix into cream cheese mixture. Divide mixture among ramekins.

3 Refrigerate until set. Run a knife around the edge of the ramekin. Turn onto serving plates. Serve garnished with apple slices and toasted coconut.

Serves 8

Super Quick Biscotti Cheesecakes

125g cream cheese

1 tablespoon orange flavoured liqueur

2 tablespoons strawberry jam

16 pieces almond biscotti

8 large strawberries

¼ cup chocolate sauce

1 Soften cream cheese. Mix cream cheese, liqueur and jam together.

2 Spread thickly over biscotti.

3 Top with strawberries and drizzle over chocolate sauce.

Serves 6–8

Lemon Ricotta Cheesecake

55g butter

100g digestive biscuits, crushed

45g ground almonds

3 lemons

250g ricotta

145g plain yoghurt

3 eggs

1 tablespoon cornflour

75g caster sugar

1 tablespoon clear honey

1 Preheat the oven to 180°C. Melt the butter in a saucepan, then stir in the biscuits and almonds. Press into the base of a deep, lightly greased 20cm loose-bottomed cake tin. Cook in the oven for 10 minutes.

2 Meanwhile, finely grate the zest from 2 of the lemons and squeeze the juice. Blend with the ricotta, yoghurt, eggs, cornflour and sugar in a food processor until smooth, or beat with a hand whisk. Pour the mixture over the biscuit base and bake for 45–50 minutes, until lightly set and golden. Cool in the tin for at least 1 hour, then run a knife around the edge to loosen and turn out onto a serving plate.

3 Thinly slice the remaining lemon. Place it in a saucepan, cover with boiling water and simmer for 5 minutes, then drain. Heat the honey over a low heat – but don't let it boil. Dip the lemon slices in the honey and arrange them over the cheesecake.

Serves 6

Note: This light and lemony cheesecake with a biscuit and almond base is simple to make. It can be served either as a dessert or with coffee as a sweet treat.

Walnut and Date Cheesecake

250g digestive biscuits

75g butter

FILLING

1 cup chopped dates

¼ cup boiling water

¼ cup brown sugar

2 tablespoons honey

3 eggs

1 teaspoon vanilla essence

500g cream cheese

TOPPING

1 cup chopped dates

1 cup toasted walnuts

½ cup honey

1 Crush biscuits until fine crumbs. Melt butter and mix into biscuits. Press into the base of a baking-paper-lined 20cm loose-bottom cake tin. Pour in filling.

2 Bake at 180°C for 1 hour. Cool then pour over topping.

FILLING

1 Place dates, water, sugar and honey in a bowl. Leave until cool.

2 Place date mixture, eggs and vanilla in the bowl of a food processor with cream cheese. Process until cream cheese is mixed in.

TOPPING

1 Mix dates, walnuts and honey together until combined.

Serves 8–10

American Pumpkin and Pinenut Cheesecake

250g packet vanilla wine biscuits

¼ cup pinenuts

100g butter

½ cup pinenuts

¼ cup honey

FILLING

250g cream cheese

½ cup sugar

2 cups cooked, drained, mashed
  pumpkin

1 teaspoon grated lemon rind

2 tablespoons lemon juice

1 teaspoon ground nutmeg

3 eggs

½ cup cream

PUMPKIN CREAM SAUCE

150ml cream

½ cup cooked, drained, mashed
  pumpkin

1 tablespoon icing sugar

¼ teaspoon ground nutmeg

1 Process biscuits and first measure of pinenuts in the bowl of a food processor until fine crumbs. Melt butter and mix in. Spread mixture into the base of a 20cm springform baking tin.

2 Pour in filling. Sprinkle over second measure of pinenuts. Bake at 160°C for 1½ hours or until an inserted skewer comes out clean.

3 Melt honey and brush over cheesecake. Serve at room temperature with pumpkin cream sauce.

FILLING

1 Soften cream cheese and beat with sugar until smooth. Mix in pumpkin, lemon rind, juice and nutmeg until combined. Separate eggs. Beat egg yolks into mixture. Beat egg whites until stiff. Whip cream until soft peaks form. Fold egg whites and cream into pumpkin mixture.

PUMPKIN CREAM SAUCE

1 Whip cream until soft peaks form. Fold in pumpkin, icing sugar and nutmeg.

Serves 6–8

Christmas Mincemeat Cheesecake

250g packet digestive biscuits

75g butter

FILLING

250g cream cheese

4 eggs

250g plain cottage cheese

½ cup sugar

¼ cup cornflour

1 cup Christmas mincemeat

2 tablespoons icing sugar

1 Crush biscuits until coarse crumbs. Melt butter and mix into crumbs. Press over the base of a 20cm round springform tin. Pour in filling.

2 Bake at 200°C for 10 minutes then reduce heat to 180°C and cook for a further 35 to 40 minutes or until set.

3 Leave to cool in tin, then remove carefully. Serve warm or at room temperature, dusted with icing sugar.

FILLING

1 Soften cream cheese. Separate eggs. Beat cream cheese, cottage cheese, sugar, cornflour and egg yolks together until smooth. Beat egg whites until stiff. Fold cheese mixture into egg whites with mincemeat.

Serves 8–10

New York Cheesecake

12 digestive biscuits

½ cup blanched almonds

¼ cup sugar

50g butter

FILLING

750g cream cheese

½ cup sugar

1 tablespoon lemon juice

2 teaspoons grated lemon rind

4 eggs

1   Place biscuits, almonds and sugar in the bowl of a food processor and process until fine crumbs. Alternatively crush biscuits and finely chop almonds. Melt butter and mix into crumb mixture. Press into the base of a 20cm springform tin. Pour in filling.

2   Bake at 160°C for 55 to 60 minutes or until set. Cool and serve with fruit.

FILLING

1   Beat cream cheese, sugar, lemon juice, rind and eggs together until well combined.

Serves 8–10

chocolate heaven

Hot Chocolate Soufflé

(see photograph on page 94)

30g unsalted butter, plus extra
   for greasing

145g dark chocolate, broken
   into chunks

6 large eggs, separated

75g caster sugar

2 tablespoons cornflour

1 cup semi-skimmed milk

icing sugar to dust

1   Place a baking sheet in the oven and preheat to 200°C. Lightly butter a 1½ litre soufflé dish. Melt the chocolate with the butter in a bowl placed over a saucepan of simmering water.

2   Whisk the egg yolks and caster sugar in a large bowl until pale and fluffy. Blend the cornflour with 1 tablespoon of the milk. Heat the remaining milk in a pan, add the cornflour mixture and bring to the boil, stirring. Cook for 1 minute or until thickened. Remove from the heat and stir into the egg mixture with the melted chocolate, combining thoroughly.

3   Whisk the egg whites until they form stiff peaks (this is best done with an electric whisk). Fold a spoonful of egg white into the chocolate mixture to loosen, then gently fold in the rest. Spoon into the dish and place on the heated baking sheet. Cook for 35 minutes or until well risen. Dust with icing sugar and serve immediately.

Serves 4

Note: This soufflé is very light but has an incredible chocolate taste. People often think soufflés are difficult to make, but once you've had a go, you'll wonder what all the fuss is about.

Little Pots of Chocolate

(see photograph opposite)

200g high quality dark chocolate,
   broken into squares

⅗ cup milk

2 tablespoons brandy

1 egg

2 egg yolks

1 teaspoon vanilla extract

250ml double cream

2 tablespoons caster sugar

4 tablespoons plain yoghurt

grated nutmeg to decorate

1   Preheat the oven to 160°C. Place the chocolate, milk and brandy in a small saucepan. Cook over a low heat, stirring occasionally, for 5–6 minutes, until just melted – don't let it boil. Remove from the heat.

2   In a bowl, beat the egg, egg yolks, vanilla extract, cream and sugar until evenly combined. Quickly add to the chocolate mixture, mixing until smooth.

3   Divide the mixture evenly between 4 x 200ml ramekins. Place on a double layer of newspaper in a roasting tin and pour in just enough boiling water to reach halfway up the sides of the dishes. Bake for 35–40 minutes or until lightly set. Remove and leave to cool for 30 minutes, then place in the fridge for 1 hour. Top with the yoghurt and grated nutmeg to serve.

Serves 4

Note: These little pots are made up of a gloriously rich and Italian chocolate custard. They're a real treat served with, crisp almond biscuits.

Sticky Chocolate and Raspberry Slice

75g unsalted butter, plus extra
  for greasing

75g dark chocolate, broken
  into chunks

75g fresh or frozen raspberries,
  defrosted if frozen, plus extra to
  decorate

2 medium eggs, separated

55g caster sugar

30g ground almonds

30g cocoa powder, sifted

30g plain flour, sifted

icing sugar to dust
  fresh mint to decorate

SAUCE

145g fresh or frozen raspberries,
  defrosted if frozen

1 tablespoon caster sugar (optional)

1 Preheat the oven. Grease the base and sides of an 18cm loose-bottomed cake tin and line with baking paper. Melt the chocolate and butter in a bowl set over a saucepan of simmering water, stirring. Cool slightly.

2 Meanwhile, press 75g of the raspberries through a sieve. Whisk the egg yolks and caster sugar until pale and creamy, then mix in the almonds, cocoa, flour, melted chocolate and sieved raspberries.

3 Whisk the egg whites until they form stiff peaks (this is best done with an electric whisk). Fold a little into the chocolate mixture to loosen, then fold in the remainder. Spoon into the tin and cook for 25 minutes or until risen and just firm. Cool for 1 hour.

4 To make the sauce, sieve the raspberries, then stir in the sugar (if using). Remove the cake from the tin and dust with the icing sugar. Serve with the sauce, decorated with the mint and raspberries.

Serves 6

Note: This pudding is a real show-stopper. The flavour of the raspberries mingles with the intensely chocolate cake. Serve with a dollop of crème fraîche or plain yoghurt.

Chocolate Bread and Butter Pudding

1 tablespoon butter

200g day-old fruit bread or sultana
   bread, sliced

2 tablespoon chocolate and hazelnut
   spread

2 large eggs

1⅓ cup half-fat milk

3 tablespoons double cream

1 tablespoon sugar (optional)

3 drops vanilla extract

icing sugar to dust

1   Preheat the oven to 180°C. Use a little of the butter to grease a 23 x 15cm
    ovenproof baking dish.

2   Cover 1 side of each bread slice with chocolate and hazelnut spread and
    cut into triangles if large. Layer the bread, chocolate-side up, in the dish and
    dot with the remaining butter.

3   Beat the eggs, then beat in the milk, cream, sugar (if using) and vanilla
    extract. Pour over the bread and leave to stand for 10 minutes before baking.
    Cook for 35–40 minutes, until well risen and slightly crispy on top. Lightly
    dust with icing sugar.

Serves 4

*Note: If you like bread and butter pudding and you like chocolate, you'll
love this. For a change, use panettone – Italian Christmas bread – instead
of fruit bread.*

Chocolate and Strawberry Roulade

sunflower spread for greasing

3 medium eggs

125g caster sugar

55g wholemeal flour

55g plain flour, sifted

1 tablespoon cocoa powder, sifted, plus
  2 teaspoons to dust

125g plain yoghurt

100g ricotta cheese

145g strawberries, sliced or chopped

icing sugar to dust

1 Preheat the oven to 200°C. Grease a 33 x 23cm swiss roll tin and line with non-stick baking paper. Put the eggs and caster sugar into a heatproof bowl over a saucepan of simmering water and whisk until pale and creamy. Remove from the heat and whisk until cool.

2 Lightly fold the wholemeal flour into the mixture using a metal spoon, then fold in the white flour and cocoa powder with 1 tablespoon of hot water. Pour into the tin and smooth the surface with the back of a spoon.

3 Bake for 10–12 minutes, until risen and firm. Turn out onto a sheet of non-stick baking paper, trim the edges of the sponge with a sharp knife and roll up with the paper inside. Place seam-side down on a wire rack and leave to cool for 30 minutes, then carefully unroll and discard the paper.

4 Mix together the yoghurt and ricotta and spread evenly over the cake. Scatter over the strawberries, then roll up the cake. Dust with cocoa powder and icing sugar.

Serves 6

Note: Fresh raspberries or sliced peaches, pears or bananas can also be used to fill this irresistibly light chocolate sponge.

Chocolate Puddings with Ginger Cream

unsalted butter for greasing

200g high quality chocolate, broken into pieces

1 teaspoon ground ginger

1 teaspoon vanilla extract

4 large eggs, separated

145g caster sugar

2 tablespoons plain flour

⅛ teaspoon baking powder

icing sugar for dusting

GINGER CREAM

1 cup whipping cream

1 tablespoon ginger cordial, chilled

1 teaspoon ground ginger

icing sugar to taste

1. Butter a 6 x 10cm ovenproof soufflé dishes. Refrigerate for 20 minutes. Place the chocolate in a bowl set over a pan of simmering water. Stir until melted, then stir in the ginger and vanilla extract.

2. Preheat the oven to 190°C. Remove the soufflé dishes from the refrigerator and butter again. Whisk the egg yolks into the chocolate mixture, then fold in the caster sugar, flour and baking powder with a metal spoon. Whisk the egg whites until stiff (this is easiest with an electric whisk). Fold a spoonful into the mixture to loosen it, then fold in the remainder. Spoon the mixture into the dishes and cook for 20 minutes or until well risen.

3. Meanwhile, make the ginger cream. Whip the cream until it forms soft peaks. Fold in the ginger cordial and ground ginger and sweeten to taste with icing sugar. Dust the puddings with icing sugar and serve warm with the ginger cream.

Serves 6

Note: These little puddings are firm on the outside but really light and moist on the inside. They're perfect served with a generous dollop of ginger flavoured cream.

Chocolate Mousse Cake

5 eggs

¾ cup sugar

100g cooking chocolate

100g butter

chocolate curls

1 Separate eggs. Beat egg yolks and sugar until pale, thick and creamy and mixture holds its shape.

2 Beat egg whites until stiff. Beat in sugar until thick and glossy. Melt chocolate and butter and beat into egg yolk mixture. Fold this into egg whites.

3 Baking-paper-line the bottom of a 20 x 30cm sponge roll tin and pour one-third of mixture into tin.

4 Bake at 160°C for 35 minutes or until set. Cool. Pour remaining mixture on top of cooked cake and freeze until firm. Garnish with chocolate curls and serve with whipped cream.

Serves 6–8

Chocolate Self-Saucing Pudding

1 cup plain flour

1 teaspoon baking powder

¼ cup cocoa powder

¾ cup caster sugar

½ cup milk

45g butter, melted

SAUCE

¾ cup brown sugar

¼ cup cocoa powder, sifted

1¼ cups hot water

1   Sift together the flour and cocoa powder in a bowl. Add the caster sugar and mix to combine. Make a well in the centre of the dry ingredients, add the milk and butter and mix well to combine. Pour the mixture into a greased 4 cup capacity ovenproof dish.

2   To make the sauce, place the brown sugar and cocoa powder in a bowl. Gradually add the water and mix until smooth. Carefully pour the sauce over the mixture in the dish and bake at 180°C for 40 minutes or until the cake is cooked when tested with a skewer. Serve scoops of pudding with some of the sauce from the base of the dish and top with a scoop of vanilla or chocolate ice cream.

Serves 6

Caramel Brownie with Chocolate Bar Sauce

250g butter

½ cup golden syrup

1 cup brown sugar

4 eggs

1 teaspoon baking soda

1¼ cups flour

2 teaspoons vanilla essence

1 Mars bar

2 tablespoons cream

1 Melt butter, golden syrup and brown sugar in a saucepan large enough to mix all the ingredients. Cool slightly. Beat in eggs with a wooden spoon. Beat in baking soda. Sift flour into mixture and mix in with vanilla essence.

2 Pour mixture into a baking-paper-lined 20 x 30cm sponge roll tin. Bake at 180°C for 25 to 30 minutes or until brownie springs back when lightly touched.

3 Roughly chop chocolate bar. Place in a saucepan and heat gently with the cream until melted. Spread over brownie. Cool before cutting.

Serves 8–10

Tiramisu

250g mascarpone

½ cup double cream

2 tablespoons brandy

¼ cup sugar

2 tablespoons instant coffee powder

1½ cups boiling water

250g sponge fingers

250g grated chocolate

1   Place the mascarpone, cream, brandy and sugar in a bowl, mix to combine and set aside. Dissolve the coffee powder in the boiling water and set aside.

2   Line the base of an 20cm square dish with ⅓ of the sponge fingers. Sprinkle ⅓ of the coffee mixture over the sponge fingers, then top with ⅓ of the mascarpone mixture. Repeat the layers, finishing with a layer of mascarpone mixture. Sprinkle with the grated chocolate and chill for 15 minutes before serving.

Serves 4

Note: Mascarpone is a fresh cheese made from cream. It's available from delicatessens and some supermarkets. If unavailable, mix 1 part sour cream with 3 parts lightly whipped double cream.

Pink and White Mousse

500g mixed berries of your choice

1 cup sugar

1 tablespoon orange-flavoured liqueur

¼ cup water

6 egg yolks

200g white chocolate, melted

2 teaspoons vanilla extract

1⅔ cup double thickened cream, whipped

white chocolate curls

1 Place the berries in a food processor or blender and process to make a purée. Press the purée through a sieve into a saucepan. Stir in ⅓ cup of the sugar and the liqueur and bring to simmering over a low heat. Simmer, stirring occasionally, until the mixture reduces to 1 cup. Remove the pan from the heat and set aside.

2 Place the water, egg yolks and the remaining sugar in a heatproof bowl set over a saucepan of simmering water and beat for 8 minutes or until the mixture is light and creamy. Remove the bowl from the pan. Add the chocolate and the vanilla extract and beat until the mixture cools. Fold the cream into the chocolate mixture. Divide the mixture into 2 portions.

3 Stir the berry purée into 1 portion of mixture and leave 1 portion plain. Drop alternate spoonfuls of the berry and plain mixtures into serving glasses. Using a skewer, swirl the mixtures to give a ripple effect. Refrigerate until firm. Just prior to serving, decorate with the chocolate curls.

Serves 8

Note: Garnish with fresh berries or red and white currants when available.

index